Would you like to join exciting expeditions to London and Rome?

The characters accompanying you, Joseph Richards, Dr. Helen Jones and Dr. Lorena Di Caprio, are fictional. But real facts about museums, archaeologists and scientists have been used to give you an accurate picture of the work they do. The Roman gladiator that you will help to investigate is also fictional. But the characteristics of the gladiator and details about life in Roman times are based on real discoveries made by archaeologists.

Interested to know more? Ready to dig for ancient clues?

Then welcome to the City Museum...

CONTENTS

A ROMAN PUZZLE	4
JOINING THE PIECES	6
A GLADIATOR'S GRAVE	8
MAKING ANCIENT FACES	10
THE ROMAN EMPIRE	12
AT THE COLOSSEUM	14
INSIDE THE COLOSSEUM	16
A DAY AT THE GAMES	18
SCHOOL FOR GLADIATORS	20
UNDER THE MICROSCOPE	22
THE GLADIATOR'S SECRET	24
HADRIAN'S WALL	26
THE MUSEUM EXHIBITION	28
GLOSSARY	30
INDEX	32

CITY MUSEUM PASS

Name: Dr. Helen Jones
Department: Head of Ancient Greek and Roman Antiquities

Interests: Ancient civilizations, digging, travel and scuba-diving.

CITY MUSEUM PASS

Name: Joseph Richards
Department: Ancient Greek and Roman Antiquities — temporary research assistant

Interests: Ancient history, computers and movies.

TEMPORARY

Day 1

What a brilliant way to spend the summer. The City Museum asked for volunteers to help sort out their storeroom, and I was picked! I never thought I'd get the chance to find out what goes on behind the scenes at a museum. The storeroom is packed with items donated to the museum or excavated (dug up) by the museum's archaeologists. Most of the things found by the archaeologists go into storage. Only the really good stuff goes on display!

I'm working with Dr. Helen Jones the curator, or head, of the department of ancient Greek and Roman antiquities. Earlier today Dr. Jones asked if I'd like to clean some Roman pottery that had been given to the museum. No-one knows where the pottery was originally found, but it needed to be washed and sorted before it could go into storage. Dr. Jones tipped one of the boxes of broken pottery pieces onto the workbench. She said to clean the edges carefully because if any of the pieces matched up, we could try sticking them back together.

A Roman leather sandal. It is quite rare to find an artefact made from a perishable material like leather, but sometimes items survive if they are buried in waterlogged ground.

An archaeologist is a scientist who investigates human life in the past. They study everyday items and buildings that have been excavated.

Excavations at Roman sites mostly find pottery. Pieces of broken pottery from archaeological digs are known as 'potsherds'.

Roman potters who made this type of red pottery, called 'terra sigillata', often stamped their names onto the pots.

Potsherds come out of the ground looking very dirty. They're cleaned in water, using ordinary toothbrushes and nailbrushes, then laid out in trays to dry.

A gold Roman armlet. Gold doesn't corrode or decay. Pieces of gold jewellery can survive buried in the ground or even underwater for thousands of years – and still look like new!

From: Joseph Richards, The City Museum
To: City School History Club
Subject: A Roman jigsaw puzzle

Hi guys,

Here I am at the City Museum, and guess what I've been doing – the washing-up! Only joking. I've been 'pot washing', and I've found something really interesting. Amongst the 'potsherds' were some pieces of shiny red pottery. My boss, Dr. Jones, said the Romans called it 'terra sigillata', but people today call it 'Samian ware'. In Roman times this type of pottery was mass-produced in factories. It was made into drinking cups, bowls and platters, and was considered very fashionable. Dr. Jones says the pieces have come from a particular design of bowl that was made in France between AD 130 and AD 150. When I pointed out some little decorations of men fighting and some strange marks on the pottery, Dr. Jones got really excited. She said the marks were Latin writing, and she would try to decipher them.

Day 10

It turns out the men fighting on the Samian ware bowl are Roman gladiators! One of the museum conservators (that's someone who repairs and restores things) joined the pieces of Samian ware pottery back together, then filled in the missing parts with modelling clay. It was like doing a jigsaw. Slowly a Roman bowl appeared. It showed a gladiator with a trident (Dr. Jones said he was a 'retiarius') fighting a gladiator with a shield and a sword (a 'secutor'). Many different types of gladiator fought in ancient Rome, and they all used different kinds of weapons. Best of all, Dr. Jones could read the name of the gladiator who once owned the bowl. The scratchy Latin writing (which Dr. Jones called a 'graffito') is his stage name. It says 'Triumphus Naso'. In English it means 'Triumphus Big Nose'!

A newspaper reporter has just been to interview Dr. Jones. He is going to write a story about our discovery.

'Gladiator' is my favourite DVD. Dr. Jones tells me that many gladiators were criminals, but some were sold into slavery like Maximus (Russell Crowe) in the movie.

We've unpacked some gladiator artefacts from the museum's collection. These little pottery gladiators were given as gifts during Saturnalia, a Roman festival in celebration of the new year. They were found in a tomb.

Like some actors and popstars today, Roman gladiators used stage names.

TRIVMPHVS NASO

The conservator glued the potsherds back together, and filled in the gaps with clay, coloured to match the pot.

A heavy bronze helmet worn by a type of gladiator called a 'Thracian'. The helmet was effective protection for the head, but made it hard for the wearer to see where he was going!

GLADIATOR WITH A 'NOSE' FOR A FIGHT

Archaeologists at the City Museum have unveiled their latest find. The Roman Samian ware bowl that went on show yesterday was discovered after a young assistant was given the task of cleaning a box of broken pieces of pottery. Now experts are hailing the bowl, which is decorated with images of gladiators, as one of the most important finds in years because it has the name of its Roman owner scratched on it. Dr. Helen Jones said 'It belonged to a gladiator who fought under the stage name of "Triumphus Naso", which means Triumphus Big Nose.' Dr Jones hopes to find out more about this gladiator, who clearly had a 'nose' for a fight.

From: Dr. Paul Dixon, London
To: Dr. Helen Jones, The City Museum
Subject: Roman cemetery excavation

Dear Helen,

Congratulations to you and your team on your recent work on the 'Gladiator bowl'. I read the newspaper article with interest, and am pleased to say that I have some exciting news for you. My team has recently been excavating a Roman cemetery. It was discovered during development work for a new office building, and lies just outside the old Roman walls of London. As you know, Roman cemeteries were always built on the outskirts of towns – never where people lived. We have discovered a mixture of cremations (burial urns containing ashes) and inhumations (graves with bones and grave goods), but yesterday one of my colleagues uncovered something that I think will really interest you. How quickly can you come to London?

A GLADIATOR'S GRAVE

Day 15

Here we are in London. I was so excited when Dr. Jones said I could come along as her research assistant. It has taken the London archaeologists many weeks to excavate the Roman cemetery. An accurate drawing of every grave has been made and lots of photographs taken. Sometimes the archaeologists map out areas of the dig site using pegs with string stretched across to make a large grid. Then they draw a corresponding grid on paper, just like a map. This 'map' is used to record the position of all the 'finds' (objects uncovered on the site) before they are moved.

We joined the archaeologists alongside one of the graves. About half a metre down in the damp soil was a skeleton and, close-by, a marble grave marker. I couldn't believe it when I saw the words 'Triumphus Naso'. Dr. Jones translated the Latin inscription for me: "Marcus Licinius, Triumphus Big Nose, retiarius, is buried here". So, Triumphus, whose real name was Marcus Licinius, was a retiarius.
But how did a Roman gladiator come to be buried in London?

The dig site is in the business area of London, amongst the office blocks. We drove over the famous Tower Bridge to get there.

The archaeologists have dug their hole by following the size and shape of the original grave. The wooden coffin and fabric shroud (the cloth that the body was wrapped in) have rotted away, leaving just the bones and non-organic (non-living) items, like pottery.

One of the archaeologists records the contents of a grave on a 'grid map'.

Archaeologists use similar equipment to builders. A theodolite (above) takes measurements of vertical and horizontal angles.

The archaeologists remove the soil from around the skeleton's bones with small trowels and brushes. They are careful not to move the bones until they have been drawn and photographed.

Archaeologists call this 'concretion'. Possibly a metal artefact has rusted in the ground and reacted to the soil. The metal and soil have fused into a hard lump.

A pottery lamp for burning olive oil has been found in the grave. Lamps like these were used to light Roman homes. The design shows gladiators fighting.

Some Roman coins are buried close to the skeleton.

MARCVS LICINIVS
TRIVMPHVS NASO RETIARIVS
HIC SITVS EST

A retiarius fought using a dagger, a three-pronged spear called a 'trident' and a net. He threw the net over his opponent or used it to trip him.

Archaeologists wear hard hats to protect their heads from falling stones and collapsing trenches.

MAKING ANCIENT FACES

Day 16

We are going to get a chance to see what Triumphus might have looked like when he was alive! The skeleton and grave goods are going to a museum in London, and in one of their laboratories Triumphus's face will be recreated. Facial reconstruction is a fascinating procedure that enables archaeologists to rebuild ancient faces. Sometimes it is used by forensic scientists in criminal investigations to help identify the skeletal remains of murder victims.

We went along to meet the medical artist who will work on our skull, and she explained how they make such lifelike faces. A copy of the real skull is made in resin, then it is covered in clay to represent muscle and flesh. Some areas of the face like the eyes, mouth, ears and tip of the nose are difficult to reconstruct because there is no underlying bone structure. But the medical artist who works on our skull will have some useful evidence to help her rebuild Triumphus's face: the gladiator's nickname!

A medical artist paints on the skin colour to make the skull look as lifelike as possible.

False eyes and wigs are added to reconstructed skulls. Medical artists use clues from burial sites and information about where the subject came from to work out the most likely skin and hair colour.

Pioneering medical artist Richard Neave has reconstructed ancient faces from skulls found in archaeological excavations across the world. His famous subjects include bog bodies, like Lindow Man and Yde Girl, and rulers of the ancient world, such as Philip II of Macedon (father of Alexander the Great) and King Midas of Phrygia (an ancient kingdom in what is now Turkey).

RECREATING A FACE

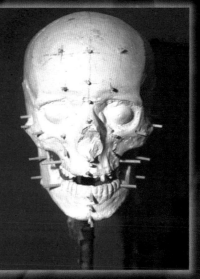

RESIN SKULL

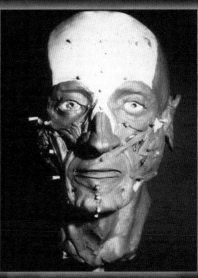

SKULL COVERED IN CLAY

1. A laser beam scans the real skull. It takes lots of accurate measurements; these are used to make a replica skull out of resin.

2. The average depths of facial tissue are well known at a number of places on human skulls. These standard measurements are used as a starting point. Wooden pegs are fixed into the replica skull to represent how thick the flesh should be in that place.

3. The skull is covered with clay to the depth of the pegs to represent muscle, flesh and skin. False eyes are added.

4. The clay is smoothed, to make it look like skin, and the finished head is painted.

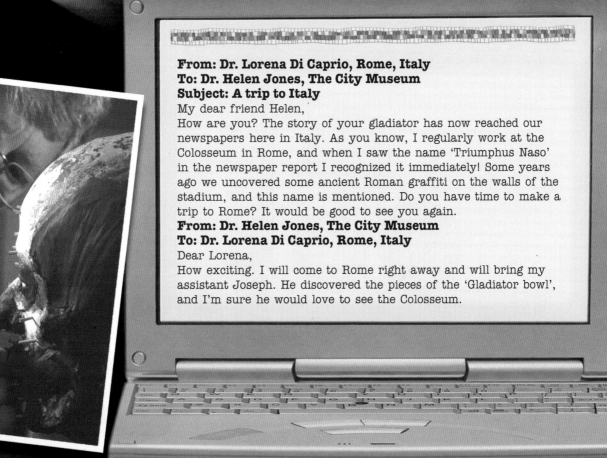

From: Dr. Lorena Di Caprio, Rome, Italy
To: Dr. Helen Jones, The City Museum
Subject: A trip to Italy
My dear friend Helen,
How are you? The story of your gladiator has now reached our newspapers here in Italy. As you know, I regularly work at the Colosseum in Rome, and when I saw the name 'Triumphus Naso' in the newspaper report I recognized it immediately! Some years ago we uncovered some ancient Roman graffiti on the walls of the stadium, and this name is mentioned. Do you have time to make a trip to Rome? It would be good to see you again.
From: Dr. Helen Jones, The City Museum
To: Dr. Lorena Di Caprio, Rome, Italy
Dear Lorena,
How exciting. I will come to Rome right away and will bring my assistant Joseph. He discovered the pieces of the 'Gladiator bowl', and I'm sure he would love to see the Colosseum.

THE ROMAN EMPIRE

Day 18

Archaeologists are just like detectives; they have to hunt for clues and then piece together a story. Our investigation of Triumphus is now taking us from London to Rome, across the Roman Empire.

The city-state of Rome was founded in around 753 BC. Its inhabitants were a mixture of Etruscans, who ruled over most of Italy, and Latins, from southern Italy. Together they became known as Romans. Rome overpowered her neighbours and took control of the whole of Italy. Then, over the course of the next 900 years the Romans invaded a large part of Europe, the Near East and parts of North Africa. Sometimes they met resistance from local tribes, but most people in the conquered countries adjusted to their new way of life. The Romans allowed them to live pretty much as they had before, and this led to a mixing of native and Roman cultures in many areas.

Hadrian's Wall, in Britain, marked the northern boundary of the Roman Empire. It was built to keep out the unconquered Caledonians or barbarians. The wall is 135 km long.

Today it takes a plane less than three hours to fly the 1,750 km from London to Rome. In Roman times, when people travelled over land on foot or by horse, the same journey would have taken about three weeks!

I mustn't get my Euros for the trip muddled up with these old Roman coins in Dr. Jones's office. Euros can be used in 12 different European countries, just as in Roman times when Roman coins could be used throughout the empire.

A Roman Centurion (army officer). The successful expansion of the Roman Empire was down to the super-efficient Roman army. The legionaries (foot soldiers) were organized into highly trained, well-disciplined legions of 5,000 men.

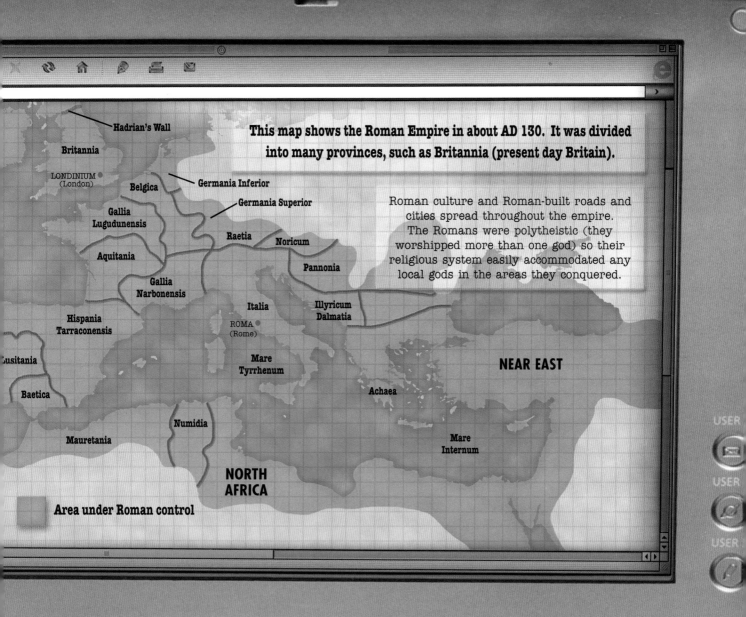

This map shows the Roman Empire in about AD 130. It was divided into many provinces, such as Britannia (present day Britain).

Hadrian's Wall

Britannia

LONDINIUM
(London)

Belgica

Germania Inferior

Germania Superior

Gallia
Lugudunensis

Raetia

Noricum

Aquitania

Pannonia

Gallia
Narbonensis

Italia

Illyricum
Dalmatia

Hispania
Tarraconensis

ROMA
(Rome)

Lusitania

Mare
Tyrrhenum

NEAR EAST

Baetica

Achaea

Numidia

Mare
Internum

Mauretania

NORTH
AFRICA

Area under Roman control

Roman culture and Roman-built roads and cities spread throughout the empire. The Romans were polytheistic (they worshipped more than one god) so their religious system easily accommodated any local gods in the areas they conquered.

Today Europe and the surrounding regions are made up of independent countries. It is interesting to compare a modern map (below) with a map of the Roman Empire in Triumphus's time (as above).

From: Dr. Lorena Di Caprio, Rome, Italy
To: Joseph Richards, The City Museum
Subject: Your trip to Italy

Dear Joseph,
I'm very glad that you can make the trip to Italy. Please don't worry that you can't speak any Italian – I will be happy to help you. In Roman times it was easier. Latin was the official language throughout the empire. People who spoke and wrote Latin were understood from London to Rome. Triumphus probably knew Latin, though it may not have been his first language. If he was a slave he could have been captured from anywhere in the Roman Empire. When he became a gladiator he would have learned Latin and been given his Roman names. I hope the trip will throw some light on Triumphus's secrets! See you tomorrow – ciao.

The Colosseum measures 188 m x 156 m across the base. It stands about 50 m high – roughly the same height as a 12–15 storey building.

Day 19

We were met by Dr. Di Caprio at Fiumicino airport in Rome. First we would have a quick tour of the city, then a delicious Italian dinner! Tomorrow we would see inside the Colosseum. Rome is the capital city of Italy. It was built on seven hills overlooking the River Tiber. At first Rome was just a cluster of small villages, but eventually they grew into this great city. This historian's version of what happened is fairly accurate, but isn't as exciting as the ancient Roman myth in my guidebook!

As we ate our meal, Dr. Di Caprio explained that the Romans built huge open-air buildings called 'amphitheatres' in most of their towns. They were used to stage plays, sporting events and gladiatorial contests. It took Roman builders about ten years to build the Colosseum; it opened in AD 80 and was in use for 400 years. I tried to imagine how it must have looked when it was a working building as thousands of excited, noisy spectators arrived to watch gladiators fight to the death.

A GUIDE TO ROME

THE LEGEND OF ROMULUS AND REMUS

According to legend Rome was founded by twin brothers Romulus and Remus. They were descendants of Mars, the Roman god of war. The brothers were thrown into the River Tiber by their wicked great uncle, but were rescued by a she-wolf. A shepherd adopted them and raised them as his own. As adults they built their own city, but they couldn't decide who would be king. The brothers fought, and Romulus killed Remus. He named the new city Rome – after himself.

The Colosseum had 80 entrance and exit places. Even though it held thousands of spectators, the building could be emptied in a matter of minutes.

THE ROMULUS PIZZERIA MENU

Bowl of olives with bread

Olives were one of the main crops grown by the Romans. Olives were crushed for their oil or eaten whole as appetizers (just like today).

The Romans' main food was bread, fish and poultry with lots of fresh vegetables and fruit. The same sort of food is still eaten today in 'Mediterranean' countries like Italy and Greece.

CHOOSE FROM A WIDE SELECTION OF:

Pizzas

Pasta dishes

Fish dishes

Meat dishes

Salad and vegetables

Fresh fruit

Red or white wine

Water – sparkling or still

Both rich and poor Romans drank wine. There were black, red, yellow and white wines. Sometimes they mixed honey or herbs into the wine; this improved the taste, especially if the wine was old.

A popular Roman dessert was fresh fruit like grapes or figs.

The Romans mixed water with their wine; it was not the done thing to drink it neat!

15

Day 20

This morning we headed straight for the Colosseum. Dr. Di Caprio led us up a staircase almost to the top of the building. The view was fantastic; we could see right down to the area that had once been below the arena floor. Dr. Jones told me that when the Colosseum was first built the floor was solid, and the arena could be flooded to form an artificial lake. Sea battles were held with actual warships. In Roman times people had sat where I was sitting and had watched men (and, according to Dr. Di Caprio, even women) killing each other. To the Romans gladiator games were public entertainment, just like going to the cinema or theatre today. The big difference was that these Roman players were not acting — they were killing each other for real.

Next we went to look for the piece of ancient Roman graffiti that had excited Dr. Di Caprio so much. Scratched in the grey Roman concrete were the outlines of two gladiators, drawn like stick figures. A secutor fighting a retiarius — Triumphus.

Spectators often carved the names of their favourite gladiators into the walls of the arena. Was this done by one of Triumphus's fans?

The Colosseum had room for 50,000 spectators — 45,000 people sat on its tiers of seats, and 5,000 stood. It was very well organized and spectators were given numbered tickets for designated seats. Roman officials had the best seats, nearest the action. Women had the worst seats, at the very top of the building.

FIGHTERS OF THE ARENA

Different types of gladiators were matched against each other in fights. A *murmillo* usually fought a *thrax*, and a *retiarius* usually fought a *secutor*.

Retiarius (*net-fighter*)

Carried a net to catch his opponent. His left arm and shoulder were protected by guards. He fought with a dagger and a three-pronged trident.

Secutor (*chaser*)

Carried a large rectangular shield and wore a visored helmet. His weapon was a dagger or short sword.

Murmillo (*fish-man*)

Had a fish crest on his helmet. He carried a large shield and fought with a sword. His legs and sword-arm were protected with fabric wrappings.

Thrax (*Thracian*)

Heavily armoured. Carried a small, square shield, and fought with a very short, curved thrusting sword.

Sagittarius (*archer*)

Fought with a powerful bow, which fired arrows over distances of up to 200 m.

Andabata (*blind-fighter*)

Wore chain mail and a fully visored helmet that was closed so he couldn't see out. Found his enemy, usually another andabata, by groping blindly around then thrusting at him with a sword.

Eventually the solid floor of the Colosseum was replaced with wood covered in sand. The sand could be raked over between fights, and it soaked up the blood! The word 'arena' comes from the Latin word for sand. Beneath the arena a labyrinthine underworld of passageways and cells was built.

Later that day

Spectators took their seats early at the Colosseum, so as not to miss any of the action. The main event began after lunch. The gladiators paraded into the arena and stood in line. Raising their right arms they called out in Latin 'Ave, imperator, morituri te salutant!' (Hail, emperor, those who are about to die salute thee!). Then the fighting and the killing began. I thought about Triumphus as he said those words, each time wondering if he would live to say them again.

Before we headed back to our hotel, I wanted to have one last look around. Down in the dark maze of tunnels and cells under the Colosseum, I tried to imagine how it must have felt for the gladiators: the baying crowds above, the howling wild animals, the smell of blood, knowing you had to kill or be killed, I could almost imagine...
I decided it was time to find Dr. Jones and Dr. Di Caprio!

THE DAY'S EVENTS

Morning
Animals were killed by trained hunters, and sometimes the animals fought each other. Perfume was sprayed into the crowd to mask the smell of blood and excrement.

Lunchtime
Criminals were executed in the middle of the day. They were tied to posts in the arena to be torn to shreds by lions, tigers and leopards.

Afternoon
The main attraction — gladiatorial contests. Several pairs of gladiators would fight at the same time. Dead gladiators were carried away to the mortuary where their throats were cut to check they were really dead — survivors were patched up by doctors to fight again.

Dear Mum and Dad,
Hope you like this famous painting of a gladiator fight. The man on the ground is about to be killed by the man standing. The crowd have their thumbs turned down, which some people think was the signal for a man to die. Dr. Jones told me no-one knows if this is true; some experts think the thumbs-up sign was the death signal, not thumbs down!

'Pollice Verso' ('Thumbs Down') by Gérôme

Thousands of wild animals were brought to the Colosseum to be killed — crocodiles, lions, tigers, elephants, rhinos, bulls, hyenas and even polar bears. The animals were kept in pens beneath the arena. Hand-operated elevators were used to raise them up through trap doors in the arena floor. The Romans called animal hunts *venationes* and the animal fighters *venatores*. Sometimes archers shot animals in the arena from the safety of metal cages. Like gladiators, venatores were normally criminals or prisoners of war. They were trained to do their job, but were not as popular with the crowds as gladiators.

SCHOOL FOR GLADIATORS

Day 22

While we were in Italy I wanted to find out how gladiators were trained. Dr. Jones explained that prisoners captured in battle were sold to a 'lanista', who owned the gladiators and ran the 'ludus' (gladiator school). Once at the school, the trainee gladiators were taught how to fight by a 'magister'. When they were trained, the lanista hired out the gladiators to wealthy people.

I wanted to see what a gladiator school looked like. Dr. Jones knew a good place to visit, and after a long drive we arrived in the ancient Roman city of Pompeii. On the 24th August AD 79, just as the inhabitants of Pompeii were preparing to enjoy their midday meal, the volcano Mount Vesuvius erupted. A deluge of ash and lava completely buried the city, preserving it for all time. This terrible catastrophe has left archaeologists with a wealth of information about everyday life in Roman times. We were going to find out about the trainee gladiators of Pompeii.

Plaster casts of some unfortunate Pompeii citizens. The volcanic ash hardened around their dead bodies, and eventually the flesh and bones inside decayed leaving just a hollow shell. The archaeologist Guiseppe Fiorelli used the empty shells as moulds. He filled them with plaster of Paris, then chipped away the ash when the plaster had hardened.

The gladiator training ground at Pompeii. Trainee gladiators were taught to fight against a tall wooden post, a 'palus', and a 'man of straw', a body-shaped bag which swung from a beam. They imagined these were opponents in the arena. While in training, a gladiator did not use real equipment. He practised using a wooden sword or blunt weapons (in case he injured himself).

Dear Mum and Dad,
We are now in Pompeii. The ruins here have given us many detailed clues about life in Roman times. In 1860, an Italian archaeologist Guiseppe Fiorelli began systematically excavating and restoring the site. Mosaics and paintings were uncovered and artefacts that show bronzesmiths, butchers, bakers, goldsmiths, ironmongers, leather workers and potters all worked and traded in the city. One house even had a 'beware of the dog sign' made in mosaics!

Mount Vesuvius

Time for some lunch, more fantastic pizza and olives! Trainee gladiators ate boiled beans and barley, which was made into porridge and bread. This diet made them muscular and strong. Because they ate so much barley, gladiators were nicknamed 'hordearii' (barley men).

Gladiator barracks were a bit like army camps. In the Pompeii barracks more than 50 skeletons were found, including two who were chained up in a sort of prison cell. Spearheads and gladiator leg greaves were also uncovered.

A lot of graffiti was scrawled on the walls of the Pompeii barracks. Perhaps it was drawn by the gladiators as a way of rehearsing their moves?

SPARTACUS THE GLADIATOR IN TRAINING

Spartacus – another great film about a Roman slave who becomes a gladiator. In this scene the lanista marks out target zones on the body of Spartacus. These were the places for gladiators to aim at.

Gladiators lived, worked, slept and ate together. But when the time came to step into the arena, friendships were put aside, and they had to kill their colleagues.

Two weeks later

After the trip to Rome I felt I knew a lot more about gladiators, but there were still plenty of unanswered questions about Triumphus. He was a retiarius gladiator and he fought at the Colosseum. But how had he become a gladiator? Was he a Roman or did he come from another part of the empire? And why was he buried in London?

Some of the items from the excavation in London had been sent to the City Museum laboratory for further analysis. Soil samples collected from the grave had been washed and treated with chemicals; then they were put through a fine-mesh sieve to collect any minuscule grains of pollen. The shapeless lump of hard concretion, that was found close to the skeleton, had been X-rayed. Just as X-rays show the bones inside a body, this picture showed the object inside the concretion. It was a gladiator's dagger!

An X-ray reveals the shape of a dagger inside the lump of concretion. The conservator now knows which material is unwanted, and which is safe to remove.

Using a small drill, like the ones dentists use, the conservator carefully removed the hardened soil to reveal the dagger encased inside.

22

Pollen grains are invisible to the naked eye. These have been magnified many times. Plants produce distinctive shapes of pollen, which can be identified.

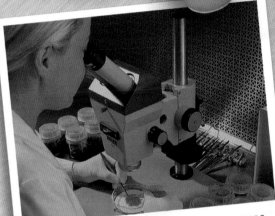

A scientist uses a powerful microscope to search for pollen grains in a soil sample taken from the gladiator's grave.

From: Joseph Richards, The City Museum
To: City School History Club
Subject: Some more evidence

Hi to everyone,

I've been helping out in the laboratory all day. I never knew that so much information could come out of ordinary dirt! A sample of the soil used to fill in Triumphus's grave has been put under a microscope, and it revealed grains of ancient pollen. Dr. Jones told me that because pollen has a tough outer shell it can survive for a very long time in the ground and is of great value to archaeologists. Plants only produce pollen at certain times of the year so archaeologists can use it as evidence for when something happened. Lots of the pollen found in Triumphus's grave came from oak trees. Oaks only release their pollen in May and June, which must mean that Triumphus probably died and was buried at this time.

Dr. Jones also told me that oak pollen is a major cause of hay fever – I wonder if Triumphus Big Nose suffered from hay fever?

USER 1

USER 2

USER 3

THE GLADIATOR'S SECRET

Scientists at work

In another part of the museum laboratory Triumphus's skeleton was being examined by a palaeopathologist (a doctor who studies old bones). Hopefully he would be able to tell us approximately how old Triumphus was when he died.

Meanwhile Dr. Jones was trying to work out when that had happened. She had one very helpful clue, the coins that the London archaeologists found in the grave. The coins showed the head of the Roman Emperor Antoninus Pius. Dr. Jones explained that Antoninus Pius reigned from AD 138 to 161. For the coins to have been buried in his grave, Triumphus must have died after AD 138. It was a useful starting point! Bit by bit we were unravelling Triumphus's story. However, we were still no nearer answering the most puzzling question of all: what was a Roman gladiator doing in London?

Right humerus

Broken ribs

The bones are a brownish-yellow colour from being in the ground for a long time.

REPORT: Roman skeleton, London excavation
Dr. Tony Scully, palaeopathologist, City Hospital

I have examined the skeleton from the excavation for signs of injury and illness, and have found that the individual (a male) had suffered the following injuries:

1. Several ribs broken, possibly from a fall or heavy blow.
2. Fractured right clavicle (collar bone). Angle of break suggests that the subject had been hit from above.
3. Fractured right humerus (bone between elbow and shoulder). Clean break. May have been caused by a powerful strike or a very heavy fall.

None of these injuries was life-threatening, and all had healed well. We can tell the subject was over 25 years old because the ends of the long bones – such as the femur (thigh bone) – were fused (joined to other bones).

Right clavicle (collar bone)

From: Dr. Paul Dixon, Hadrian's Wall
To: Dr. Helen Jones, The City Museum
Subject: Could this be your man?

Dear Helen and Joseph,

With the London dig completed, I'm now working up here in the north of England. One of the archaeologists on site has just made the most remarkable discovery at one of the Roman forts on Hadrian's Wall. They've found a Roman letter written on a wooden writing tablet. It is dated sometime around AD 135 to 145. The letter is from a man who calls himself 'Triumphus Naso'. This must be the same gladiator you've been finding out about! He's writing to his sister, who is married to a Roman soldier stationed at Hadrian's Wall. Triumphus tells his sister that he's been awarded a 'wooden sword' (he uses the Latin word 'rudis'). To be given the wooden sword meant a gladiator could retire from the arena. Triumphus says he has fought 25 times, and has lived long enough to retire. He is 'coming home' to Britain.

USER 1

USER 2

USER 3

Triumphus's story

Triumphus must have been a good gladiator to have fought 25 times and lived! Dr. Jones told me a gladiator only had about three fights a year, so Triumphus could have been a fighter for eight years before he retired. The final part of our investigation would be a trip to Hadrian's Wall, in the north of England, to see the place where Triumphus's story had begun. The evidence from the grave, the palaeopathologist's report and Triumphus's letter home tell us that Triumphus probably died sometime around AD 140, when he was about 30 to 35 years old. We've combined this information with our research into gladiators to piece together Triumphus's amazing story.

Triumphus was born a Briton, some time around AD 105 to 110. Perhaps he was from a tribe that fought the Romans, but one day he was captured. As a prisoner of war he was sent to Rome, where he was bought by a lanista and taught to fight as a retiarius gladiator. His sister, like many women in the conquered territories, met and married a Roman soldier stationed at Hadrian's Wall.

The Roman writing materials, an inkwell, pens, and wooden writing tablets, found at a fort on Hadrian's Wall. Messages were written on tablets in ink, or scratched into a thin layer of wax.

Roman soldiers began building Hadrian's Wall in AD 122, during the reign of Emperor Hadrian. It took about ten years to complete. Parts of the wall were originally made from turf and timber, but in its final state it was all made from stone. The wall is 2.4–3 m thick and 4.25–4.65 m high.

THE ROMANS IN BRITAIN

The Roman baths at Bath, in England.

The Romans understood how important hygiene, drainage systems and clean water were. Roman towns had public bath houses and toilets, and hot and cold plunge baths were very popular. The Roman name for the town of Bath, England, was Aquae Sulis (the Waters of Sulis). The Romans built baths here over a natural hot spring.

Milecastles (fortified gateways housing 8 to 32 men) were built every Roman mile. Seventeen forts were built on the wall, each housing 500 to 1,000 troops.

Although he was injured several times, Triumphus was popular with the crowds and was awarded the 'rudis'. A free man, he left Rome for Britain. But on his way home, in the spring of about AD 140, he died in London and was buried there. The cause of his death is still unknown. Dr. Jones says sometimes we can't find all the answers. As we walked along the wall, I tried to imagine Triumphus's sister waiting for news of her brother. How sad that they were never to see each other again!

Ten months later

It's incredible to think that so much could be learned about a man who died almost 2,000 years ago; but all the hardwork is not finished yet! Behind the scenes at the City Museum, Dr. Jones and a team of curators, designers, conservators, carpenters and even builders are preparing for a major new exhibition: 'The Story of a Gladiator'.

Until now everything has taken place out of sight of the public. But when the exhibition opens, the whole world will have a chance to find out about the man who was born at the edge of the Roman Empire, but went on to become a hero of the Colosseum. It's almost a year since I spent that day cleaning the pieces of Roman pottery at the museum. It's exciting to think that I played a part in tracking down the story of the man the Romans called 'Triumphus Big Nose'!

These 'Triumphus postcards' will be sold in the museum gift shop.

Triumphus fought with a short dagger, with an iron blade. It was called a **pugio**. Triumphus had brought his dagger home with him, but we don't know what happened to his other weapons, the net and three-pronged trident.

THE STORY OF A GLADIATOR

The model of Triumphus's reconstructed head is on display. Visitors can now see the face of a gladiator who lived nearly 2,000 years ago. We know Triumphus was from northern Britain so the medical artists have given him red hair and blue eyes — and of course a rather large nose!

The Samian ware bowl was made in France. Triumphus may have bought it on his way home to Britain. It was lucky that the pieces were discovered and brought into the museum.

Triumphus was buried with a pottery lamp, decorated with battling gladiators. The lamp held oil which was burned by a wick.

The marble gravemarker found at Triumphus's grave gave both his Roman name (Marcus Licinius) and the name by which he was known in the arenas of Rome — Triumphus Naso.

GLOSSARY

Amphitheatre A round or oval-shaped building with rising tiers of seats around an arena. They were often open-air, and were used by the Romans for sporting events and spectacles such as gladiator contests.

Archaeologist Someone who studies the past by examining the physical remains left behind.

Arena The floor area of an amphitheatre. Arena means 'sand' in Latin.

Artefacts Objects made by humans, for example a tool or pot. Often they are the subject of an archaeological study.

Barbarians According to the Romans, any person from outside the Roman world.

Barracks Groups of buildings where soldiers live.

Centurion An officer in the Roman army.

Concretion A hard, rocky mass formed from corroded metal and the natural material (like soil) around it.

Curator Senior member of the staff of a museum, in charge of its collections.

Emperor The ruler of the Roman Empire.

Facial reconstruction The process of making a lifelike model of a dead person's head (and face) from resin and clay. Measurements and information are taken from the original skull.

Forensic scientist Someone who uses scientific (and sometimes medical) tests and techniques to investigate crimes.

Graffiti Words or pictures scratched or painted onto a wall or other surface, normally in a public place.

Hordearii Means 'barley men' in Latin. A nickname given to gladiators because they ate so much barley!

Lanista The owner and manager of a gladiator school and a group of gladiators.

Latin The language of the Romans. People spoke and wrote Latin throughout the Roman Empire.

Legionaries Foot soldiers in the Roman army.

Legions The main units of the Roman army. Each legion was made up of 5,000 soldiers.

Ludus A school where gladiators were trained to fight.

Magister The teacher at a gladiator school.

Mortuary A room or building in which dead bodies are kept before cremation or burial.

Mosaics Small pieces of different coloured stone laid closely together to form pictures or patterns.

Myth A traditional story that includes popular beliefs or explains a practice or natural phenomena.

Palaeopathologist A doctor who studies old bones.

Plaster of Paris A white powder made from gypsum. When mixed with water it forms a quick-setting paste that is used for making casts for broken limbs and for moulds in sculpture.

Pollen The particles of dust that the male part of a flower releases to fertilize the female part.

Polytheistic Worshipping and believing in more than one god.

Potsherds The name given to bits of broken pottery found at archaeological digs.

Province A territory of the Roman Empire.

Resin A sort of hard rubbery plastic. Plants naturally secrete resin as a sticky liquid, but it can be produced artificially using chemicals.

Rudis The wooden sword given to gladiators on their retirement from the arena.

Slave A person who is owned by another person, and has to do work for them.

Terra sigillata The Roman name given to a particular type of shiny red pottery. Today it is known as Samian ware. Cups, bowls and platters were all made from terra sigillata.

Venationes Animal hunts that were held as a form of entertainment. They took place in amphitheatres in front of crowds of spectators.

Venatores Men who were trained to hunt and fight wild animals as entertainment for Roman crowds.

INDEX

A

amphitheatres 14, 30
andabata 17
animals 19
Antoninus Pius, Emperor 24
archaeologists 8, 9, 12, 20, 23, 30
arena 17, 30
armour 7

B

barracks 21, 30
Bath (Aquae Sulis) 27
bones 9, 24, 25

C

cemeteries 7, 8
centurions 12, 30
coins 12, 24
Colosseum 14, 15, 16, 17, 18, 19
concretion 9, 22, 30
conservators 6, 22

D

daggers 9, 22, 28
drainage systems 27

F

facial reconstruction 10, 11, 30
Fiorelli, Guiseppe 20
food 15, 21

G

games 16, 17

Gérôme, Jean Léon 18
Gladiator (film) 6
gladiators 6, 7, 9, 16, 17, 18
    training 20, 21
gods 13
gold 5
graffiti 6, 11, 21, 28, 30
grid maps 8

H

Hadrian's Wall 12, 13, 25, 26, 27

J

jewellery 5

L

lamps 9, 29
lanista 20, 21, 30
Latin 13, 30
leather 4
legionaries 12, 30

M

mosaics 20, 31
murmillo 17

N

Neave, Richard 10
nets 9, 17

P

palaeopathologists 24, 31
pollen 22, 23, 31
Pompeii 20

potsherds 4, 5, 31
pottery 4, 9, 29

R

Remus 14
retiarius 6, 9, 17
Roman Empire 12, 13
Rome 12, 13, 14
Romulus 14
rudis (wooden sword) 25, 31

S

sagittarius 17
Samian ware 5, 6, 7, 29
sandal 4
Saturnalia 6
secutor 6, 17
Spartacus 21

T

teeth 25
terra sigillata 4, 5, 31
thrax (Thracian) 7, 17
tridents 9, 17

V

venatores 19, 31
Vesuvius, Mount 20

W

weapons 6, 9, 17, 20, 22, 28
writing materials 26

t=top, b=bottom, c=centre, l=left, r=right, OFC=outside front cover, OBC=outside back cover

Alamy: 3br, 3bl,14-15, 19br. Corbis: 5tr, 6cr, 7t, 8tr, 8br, 12br, 14-15b, 16-17, 18-19, 18b, 19t, 20cr, 21t, 26-27, 27cr, 27bl. Desiderio Sanzi: 2-3c, 6br, 9c, 16bl. Everett Collection: 6tr. Heritage Image Collection: 9cr, 26bl. Science Photo Library: 8bc, 9l, 10-11, 20br, 23tr. University of Manchester (Unit of Art in Medicine): 11tr, 11bl.

Every effort has been made to trace the copyright holders, and we apologize in advance for any unintentional omissions. We would be pleased to insert the appropriate acknowledgements in any subsequent edition of this publication.